DreamWorks
MONSTERS
VS.
ALIENS ™
MAD LIBS®

by Roger Price and Leonard Stern

PSS!
PRICE STERN SLOAN

PRICE STERN SLOAN
Published by the Penguin Group
Penguin Group (USA) Inc., 375 Hudson Street, New York, New York 10014, USA
Penguin Group (Canada), 90 Eglinton Avenue East, Suite 700,
Toronto, Ontario M4P 2Y3, Canada
(a division of Pearson Penguin Canada Inc.)
Penguin Books Ltd., 80 Strand, London WC2R 0RL, England
Penguin Group Ireland, 25 St. Stephen's Green, Dublin 2, Ireland
(a division of Penguin Books Ltd.)
Penguin Group (Australia), 250 Camberwell Road, Camberwell, Victoria 3124, Australia
(a division of Pearson Australia Group Pty. Ltd.)
Penguin Books India Pvt. Ltd., 11 Community Centre,
Panchsheel Park, New Delhi—110 017, India
Penguin Group (NZ), 67 Apollo Drive, Rosedale, North Shore 0632, New Zealand
(a division of Pearson New Zealand Ltd.)
Penguin Books (South Africa) (Pty.) Ltd., 24 Sturdee Avenue,
Rosebank, Johannesburg 2196, South Africa

Penguin Books Ltd., Registered Offices:
80 Strand, London WC2R 0RL, England

Mad Libs format copyright © 2009 by Price Stern Sloan.

Monsters vs. Aliens ™ & © 2009 DreamWorks Animation L.L.C.

Published by Price Stern Sloan,
a division of Penguin Young Readers Group,
345 Hudson Street, New York, New York 10014.

ISBN 978-0-8431-2568-9

1 3 5 7 9 10 8 6 4 2

MAD LIBS®

INSTRUCTIONS

MAD LIBS® is a game for people who don't like games!
It can be played by one, two, three, four, or forty.

• RIDICULOUSLY SIMPLE DIRECTIONS

In this tablet you will find stories containing blank spaces where words are
left out. One player, the READER, selects one of these stories. The READER
does not tell anyone what the story is about. Instead, he/she asks the other
players, the WRITERS, to give him/her words. These words are used to fill
in the blank spaces in the story.

• TO PLAY

The READER asks each WRITER in turn to call out words—an adjective or
a noun or whatever the space calls for—and uses them to fill in the blank
spaces in the story. The result is a MAD LIBS® game.

When the READER then reads the completed MAD LIBS® game to the
other players, they will discover that they have written a story that is
fantastic, screamingly funny, shocking, silly, crazy, or just plain dumb—
depending upon which words each WRITER called out.

• EXAMPLE *(Before and After)*

" ___POOP___ !" he said _____
    EXCLAMATION   ADVERB

as he jumped into his convertible _____ and
                                            NOUN

drove off with his _____ wife.
                              ADJECTIVE

" ___Ouch___ !" he said ___Stupidly___
    EXCLAMATION   ADVERB

as he jumped into his convertible ___Cat___ and
                                            NOUN

drove off with his ___brave___ wife.
                              ADJECTIVE

MAD LIBS®

QUICK REVIEW

In case you have forgotten what adjectives, adverbs, nouns, and verbs are, here is a quick review:

An ADJECTIVE describes something or somebody. *Lumpy, soft, ugly, messy,* and *short* are adjectives.

An ADVERB tells how something is done. It modifies a verb and usually ends in "ly." *Modestly, stupidly, greedily,* and *carefully* are adverbs.

A NOUN is the name of a person, place, or thing. *Sidewalk, umbrella, bridle, bathtub,* and *nose* are nouns.

A VERB is an action word. *Run, pitch, jump,* and *swim* are verbs. Put the verbs in past tense if the directions say PAST TENSE. *Ran, pitched, jumped,* and *swam* are verbs in the past tense.

When we ask for A PLACE, we mean any sort of place: a country or city *(Spain, Cleveland)* or a room *(bathroom, kitchen).*

An EXCLAMATION or SILLY WORD is any sort of funny sound, gasp, grunt, or outcry, like *Wow!, Ouch!, Whomp!, Ick!,* and *Gadzooks!*

When we ask for specific words, like a NUMBER, a COLOR, an ANIMAL, or a PART OF THE BODY, we mean a word that is one of those things, like *seven, blue, horse,* or *head.*

When we ask for a PLURAL, it means more than one. For example, *cat* pluralized is *cats.*

MAD LIBS® is fun to play with friends, but you can also play it by yourself! To begin with, DO NOT look at the story on the page below. Fill in the blanks on this page with the words called for. Then, using the words you have selected, fill in the blank spaces in the story.

Now you've created your own hilarious MAD LIBS® game!

MY WEDDING DAY, BY SUSAN

ADJECTIVE _____

NOUN _____

ADJECTIVE _____

ADJECTIVE _____

A PLACE _____

NUMBER _____

PLURAL NOUN _____

ADJECTIVE _____

ADJECTIVE _____

ADJECTIVE _____

PART OF THE BODY _____

ADJECTIVE _____

NOUN _____

ADVERB _____

NOUN _____

ADJECTIVE _____

A PLACE _____

ADJECTIVE _____

MAD LIBS®

MY WEDDING DAY, BY SUSAN

Today's the _____ day: I'm getting married
                      ADJECTIVE

to the _____ of my life, Derek Dietl. He's the
                  NOUN

_____ weatherman for the local news *and*
       ADJECTIVE

he's a/an _____ dreamboat! I feel like the luckiest
              ADJECTIVE

woman in (the) _____. Derek and I have invited
                      A PLACE

_____ of our closest friends and _____ to
       NUMBER   PLURAL NOUN

celebrate our _____ day with us. I'm going to wear
                    ADJECTIVE

a/an _____ dress with a/an _____
          ADJECTIVE   ADJECTIVE

veil covering my _____. My _____
                  PART OF THE BODY   ADJECTIVE

dad is going to walk me down the aisle as they play "Here

Comes the _____." And Derek will be waiting
                  NOUN

_____ for me at the altar, looking as handsome
       ADVERB

as a/an _____ in his tuxedo. Finally, when the
              NOUN

_____ wedding is over, Derek will whisk me off to
       ADJECTIVE

a romantic honeymoon in (the) _____. I can't wait!
                                      A PLACE

Today is going to be the most _____ day of my life.
                                      ADJECTIVE

FROM MONSTERS VS. ALIENS™ MAD LIBS® • Monsters vs. Aliens ™ & © 2009 DreamWorks Animation L.L.C.
Published by Price Stern Sloan, a division of Penguin Young Readers Group, 345 Hudson Street, New York, NY 10014.

MAD LIBS® is fun to play with friends, but you can also play it by yourself! To begin with, DO NOT look at the story on the page below. Fill in the blanks on this page with the words called for. Then, using the words you have selected, fill in the blank spaces in the story.

Now you've created your own hilarious MAD LIBS® game!

THE MONSTER FILES: GINORMICA

NUMBER _____

ADJECTIVE _____

NOUN _____

NOUN _____

ADJECTIVE _____

ADJECTIVE _____

NUMBER _____

A PLACE _____

ADJECTIVE _____

ADVERB _____

A PLACE _____

ADJECTIVE _____

NOUN _____

PART OF THE BODY _____

ginormica

Ginormica is the most recent addition to Area __51__ .
                                                    NUMBER

This __old__ monster was a human __leg__
        ADJECTIVE   NOUN

named Susan Murphy until she was struck by a/an __monkey__
                                                  NOUN

from outer space on the day of her __spikey__ wedding.
                                      ADJECTIVE

The __slimey__ substance inside the meteorite caused
      ADJECTIVE

her to grow to the size of a/an __6__ -story building. She
                                 NUMBER

destroyed (the) __U.S.A__ , frightening the __cruvey__
                  A PLACE   ADJECTIVE

civilians in attendance. Then she was __stupidly__ captured
                                        ADVERB

and brought to (the) __Canada__ . So far, it appears there is
                      A PLACE

no cure for Ginormica's __lumpy__ condition. But a poster
                         ADJECTIVE

of a cute, cuddly __slipper__ has been placed in her cell.
                   NOUN

Hopefully that will bring a smile to her __Head__ .
                                          PART OF THE BODY

MAD LIBS® is fun to play with friends, but you can also play it by yourself! To begin with, DO NOT look at the story on the page below. Fill in the blanks on this page with the words called for. Then, using the words you have selected, fill in the blank spaces in the story.

Now you've created your own hilarious MAD LIBS® game!

DEAR DIARY

ADJECTIVE _____

ADJECTIVE _____

ADJECTIVE _____

NUMBER _____

NOUN _____

ADJECTIVE _____

NOUN _____

NOUN _____

ADJECTIVE _____

ADVERB _____

NOUN _____

MAD LIBS
DEAR DIARY

Today is my third day in this **lumpy** _____ prison that they
_____ADJECTIVE

call Area Fifty-Something. The monsters here are very kind and

Hard _____. But I don't belong here with them. I'm not a/an
___ADJECTIVE

gross _____ monster. I'm Susan—only ____**6**____ times
___ADJECTIVE   NUMBER

my normal size. I just want to get out and be with Derek, my true

Cat _____. He must really miss me. And my family must be
___NOUN

worried **slimy** _____. I can't stand being locked up in this
_____ADJECTIVE

Door _____. I hope there's a cure that will make me a normal
___NOUN

Purse _____ again. Then Derek and I can finally have our
___NOUN

Fat _____ wedding and live **lovley** _____ ever after. A
___ADJECTIVE   ADVERB

Car _____ can dream, can't she?
___NOUN

FROM MONSTERS VS. ALIENS™ MAD LIBS® • Monsters vs. Aliens ™ & © 2009 DreamWorks Animation L.L.C.
Published by Price Stern Sloan, a division of Penguin Young Readers Group, 345 Hudson Street, New York, NY 10014.

MAD LIBS® is fun to play with friends, but you can also play it by yourself! To begin with, DO NOT look at the story on the page below. Fill in the blanks on this page with the words called for. Then, using the words you have selected, fill in the blank spaces in the story.

Now you've created your own hilarious MAD LIBS® game!

LIFE IN AREA FIFTY-SOMETHING

ADJECTIVE _____

PLURAL NOUN _____

NOUN _____

VERB _____

ADJECTIVE _____

PART OF THE BODY _____

ADJECTIVE _____

ADJECTIVE _____

ADJECTIVE _____

NOUN _____

SILLY WORD _____

ADVERB _____

NOUN _____

ADJECTIVE _____

VERB _____

ADJECTIVE _____

MAD LIBS®

LIFE IN AREA FIFTY-SOMETHING

How do a bunch of _____ monsters keep themselves
                                           ADJECTIVE

entertained at Area Fifty-Something? It's not easy. And with

_____ guarding the facility like it's a maximum-security
PLURAL NOUN

_____, there's no chance of escape. Luckily, the monsters
NOUN

have one another to _____ with. They are always playing
                                     VERB

_____ pranks on one another, like the time The Missing
ADJECTIVE

Link swapped Dr. Cockroach's toothpaste for _____
                                           PART OF THE BODY

cream. They also have a/an _____ book club. It's a/an
                                    ADJECTIVE

_____ challenge for B.O.B., but it's _____
ADJECTIVE   ADJECTIVE

anyway. And they like to play board games, like Battle-_____
                                             NOUN

and _____-opoly. It gets _____ competitive,
        SILLY WORD   ADVERB

because the loser has to clean the winner's _____ for
                                           NOUN

a week. All in all, the monsters have a pretty _____
                                           ADJECTIVE

time together. But they would give anything to get out and

_____ in the _____ sunshine.
VERB   ADJECTIVE

MAD LIBS® is fun to play with friends, but you can also play it by yourself! To begin with, DO NOT look at the story on the page below. Fill in the blanks on this page with the words called for. Then, using the words you have selected, fill in the blank spaces in the story.

Now you've created your own hilarious MAD LIBS® game!

GALLAXHAR'S EVIL PLAN

PART OF THE BODY (PLURAL) _____

ADJECTIVE _____

NOUN _____

A PLACE _____

SILLY WORD _____

ADVERB _____

ADJECTIVE _____

NOUN _____

ADJECTIVE _____

ADJECTIVE _____

ADJECTIVE _____

ADJECTIVE _____

ADJECTIVE _____

MAD LIBS

GALLAXHAR'S EVIL PLAN

I, Gallaxhar, cannot wait to get my alien _____
                                            PART OF THE BODY (PLURAL)

on that _____ earthling, Susan Murphy. You see, the
            ADJECTIVE

_____ that hit her contained quantonium, the most
      NOUN

powerful substance in (the) _____. In fact, I destroyed
                                A PLACE

my home planet, _____, just so I could get to the
                    SILLY WORD

quantonium inside it. So don't doubt I'll _____ destroy
                                              ADVERB

Susan, too. If I can extract the _____ substance from her
                                    ADJECTIVE

_____, I will use it to grow big and _____,
      NOUN   ADJECTIVE

and I will once and for all take over the _____ universe.
                                              ADJECTIVE

Then I will populate it with _____ clones of myself and
                                ADJECTIVE

everyone will be as wonderful and _____ as I am. It will
                                      ADJECTIVE

be glorious! My _____ evil plan cannot be stopped!
                    ADJECTIVE

MAD LIBS® is fun to play with friends, but you can also play it by yourself! To begin with, DO NOT look at the story on the page below. Fill in the blanks on this page with the words called for. Then, using the words you have selected, fill in the blank spaces in the story.

Now you've created your own hilarious MAD LIBS® game!

SUSAN SAVES THE DAY

ADJECTIVE _____

PART OF THE BODY _____

ADJECTIVE _____

VERB (PAST TENSE) _____

ADJECTIVE _____

NOUN _____

PLURAL NOUN _____

PLURAL NOUN _____

NOUN _____

PLURAL NOUN _____

ADVERB _____

ADJECTIVE _____

PLURAL NOUN _____

NOUN _____

ADJECTIVE _____

NUMBER _____

NOUN _____

MAD LIBS®

SUSAN SAVES THE DAY

When Susan caught sight of the _____ alien robot
                                     ADJECTIVE

attacking San Francisco, she was scared out of her _____.
                                                      PART OF THE BODY

She didn't think she was _____ enough to fight it, so
                               ADJECTIVE

she _____. But when the _____ robot
        VERB (PAST TENSE)   ADJECTIVE

chased her onto the Golden Gate _____, she had no
                                          NOUN

choice but to face her _____. With some help from
                              PLURAL NOUN

her monster _____, Susan fought the robot tooth
                   PLURAL NOUN

and _____. In a matter of _____, Susan
        NOUN   PLURAL NOUN

_____ destroyed the _____ robot. She
        ADVERB   ADJECTIVE

even helped save dozens of _____ from the collapsing
                                  PLURAL NOUN

_____. Susan was amazed at her _____
        NOUN   ADJECTIVE

strength. Maybe being a _____-foot-tall _____ has
                              NUMBER   NOUN

its advantages after all!

FROM MONSTERS VS. ALIENS™ MAD LIBS® • Monsters vs. Aliens ™ & © 2009 DreamWorks Animation L.L.C.
Published by Price Stern Sloan, a division of Penguin Young Readers Group, 345 Hudson Street, New York, NY 10014.

MAD LIBS® is fun to play with friends, but you can also play it by yourself! To begin with, DO NOT look at the story on the page below. Fill in the blanks on this page with the words called for. Then, using the words you have selected, fill in the blank spaces in the story.

Now you've created your own hilarious MAD LIBS® game!

IF I ONLY HAD A BRAIN, BY B.O.B.

PLURAL NOUN _____

PART OF THE BODY (PLURAL) _____

VERB _____

ADVERB _____

PART OF THE BODY (PLURAL) _____

PLURAL NOUN _____

PLURAL NOUN _____

ADJECTIVE _____

VERB _____

VERB _____

ADJECTIVE _____

PLURAL NOUN _____

PLURAL NOUN _____

ADVERB _____

ADJECTIVE _____

ADVERB _____

MAD LIBS®
IF I ONLY HAD A BRAIN, BY B.O.B.

Most ___Poops___ have brains inside their ___Penis___
       PLURAL NOUN   PART OF THE BODY (PLURAL)

that help them think and _____. But not me! Nope,
                              VERB

I'm brainless and _____ proud of it. In fact, I think
                    ADVERB

_____ are overrated. Does anyone really
PART OF THE BODY (PLURAL)

like thinking about _____ and _____
                     PLURAL NOUN   PLURAL NOUN

anyway? I guess if I *did* have a/an _____ brain, it
                                      ADJECTIVE

might be nice to remember how to _____ or how to
                                   VERB

_____. I could probably read a/an _____
  VERB   ADJECTIVE

book about _____ or beat The Missing Link at a game
            PLURAL NOUN

of _____. And I wouldn't always get _____
    PLURAL NOUN   ADVERB

confused about who I am. Oh, no. Who am I? Oh, that's right. I'm

B.O.B. And I like not having a/an _____ brain. It makes
                                   ADJECTIVE

me _____ special!
    ADVERB

FROM MONSTERS VS. ALIENS™ MAD LIBS® • Monsters vs. Aliens ™ & © 2009 DreamWorks Animation L.L.C.
Published by Price Stern Sloan, a division of Penguin Young Readers Group, 345 Hudson Street, New York, NY 10014.

MAD LIBS® is fun to play with friends, but you can also play it by yourself! To begin with, DO NOT look at the story on the page below. Fill in the blanks on this page with the words called for. Then, using the words you have selected, fill in the blank spaces in the story.

Now you've created your own hilarious MAD LIBS® game!

THE MONSTER FILES:
INSECTOSAURUS

ADJECTIVE _____

NOUN _____

NOUN _____

NOUN _____

ADVERB _____

A PLACE _____

NOUN _____

ADJECTIVE _____

VERB _____

ADVERB _____

ADJECTIVE _____

PLURAL NOUN _____

PLURAL NOUN _____

PART OF THE BODY _____

NOUN _____

NOUN _____

MAD LIBS®
THE MONSTER FILES: INSECTOSAURUS

Insectosaurus is a/an _____ grub, or wormlike
                                ADJECTIVE

_____. _____ radiation turned him from a tiny
      NOUN   NOUN

insect into a three-hundred-and-fifty-foot-tall _____.
                                                         NOUN

He was captured after he _____ terrorized the people
                                  ADVERB

of (the) _____. Insectosaurus cannot speak, but instead
           A PLACE

communicates by screeching like a/an _____. When he
                                            NOUN

is scared or _____, he will _____. But when
                  ADJECTIVE   VERB

he is _____ upset, he is easily calmed down by a/an
              ADVERB

_____ belly rub. Insectosaurus is fascinated by bright
      ADJECTIVE

_____. He can also shoot silk _____ out of
   PLURAL NOUN   PLURAL NOUN

his _____. This enormous _____ may look
       PART OF THE BODY   NOUN

scary, but most of the time he is as gentle as a/an _____.
                                                          NOUN

MAD LIBS® is fun to play with friends, but you can also play it by yourself! To begin with, DO NOT look at the story on the page below. Fill in the blanks on this page with the words called for. Then, using the words you have selected, fill in the blank spaces in the story.

Now you've created your own hilarious MAD LIBS® game!

A WEATHER REPORT,
BY DEREK

NOUN _____

ADJECTIVE _____

ADJECTIVE _____

COLOR _____

NOUN _____

NOUN _____

ADJECTIVE _____

PLURAL NOUN _____

NUMBER _____

ADJECTIVE _____

PLURAL NOUN _____

NOUN _____

PLURAL NOUN _____

VERB _____

NOUN _____

ADJECTIVE _____

NUMBER _____

ADJECTIVE _____

MAD LIBS®
A WEATHER REPORT, BY DEREK

Good evening, Channel _____ viewers! Derek Dietl
NOUN

here with your _____ weather report. It was another
ADJECTIVE

_____ day here in Modesto, California. Nothing but
ADJECTIVE

_____ skies without a/an _____ in sight!
COLOR   NOUN

Now let's take a look at the weekend ahead. Don't forget to lather

on some _____-screen Friday, because it will be mostly
NOUN

_____ with a high of seventy-five _____.
ADJECTIVE   PLURAL NOUN

Then Saturday will be _____ degrees and partly
NUMBER

_____, with a 60 percent chance of _____.
ADJECTIVE   PLURAL NOUN

So be sure to carry a/an _____; you don't want to be
NOUN

stuck outside if it rains cats and _____! Finally, Sunday
PLURAL NOUN

looks like it will be a perfect day to _____ outdoors,
VERB

with a light _____ in the air and a/an _____,
NOUN   ADJECTIVE

cool temperature of _____ degrees. Well, that's all for me.
NUMBER

Enjoy the _____ weekend, folks!
ADJECTIVE

MAD LIBS® is fun to play with friends, but you can also play it by yourself! To begin with, DO NOT look at the story on the page below. Fill in the blanks on this page with the words called for. Then, using the words you have selected, fill in the blank spaces in the story.

Now you've created your own hilarious MAD LIBS® game!

ADDRESS TO THE NATION

ADJECTIVE _____

PERSON IN ROOM _____

A PLACE _____

NOUN _____

ADJECTIVE _____

ADJECTIVE _____

PART OF THE BODY (PLURAL) _____

ADJECTIVE _____

ADJECTIVE _____

NOUN _____

PART OF THE BODY (PLURAL) _____

NOUN _____

ADJECTIVE _____

NOUN _____

ADJECTIVE _____

TYPE OF LIQUID _____

VERB _____

PART OF THE BODY (PLURAL) _____

MAD LIBS
ADDRESS TO THE NATION

Good afternoon, _____ Americans. This is President
ADJECTIVE

_____. I am speaking to you today from (the)
PERSON IN ROOM

_____ in our nation's capital. As you may have heard, an
A PLACE

alien _____ is trying to take over our _____
NOUN   ADJECTIVE

planet. I just want to remind you to stay calm and _____.
ADJECTIVE

Our country's brightest _____ are hard at
PART OF THE BODY (PLURAL)

work trying to solve this _____ crisis. We are also
ADJECTIVE

planning to send _____ monsters to fight this alien
ADJECTIVE

_____ and bring him to his _____. Plus,
NOUN   PART OF THE BODY (PLURAL)

you have me, the bravest _____ in history. I'm not afraid
NOUN

to take _____ risks. All I have to do is press this little
ADJECTIVE

red _____ here, and that _____ alien will
NOUN   ADJECTIVE

be toast. Or, wait, maybe that's the button that makes me a hot cup

of _____. Ha-ha, guess I'll have to figure that one out.
TYPE OF LIQUID

Anyway, please _____ indoors until further notice. And
VERB

rest assured: You are in good _____.
PART OF THE BODY (PLURAL)

FROM MONSTERS VS. ALIENS™ MAD LIBS® • Monsters vs. Aliens ™ & © 2009 DreamWorks Animation L.L.C.
Published by Price Stern Sloan, a division of Penguin Young Readers Group, 345 Hudson Street, New York, NY 10014.

MAD LIBS® is fun to play with friends, but you can also play it by yourself! To begin with, DO NOT look at the story on the page below. Fill in the blanks on this page with the words called for. Then, using the words you have selected, fill in the blank spaces in the story.

Now you've created your own hilarious MAD LIBS® game!

DR. COCKROACH'S
AMAZING INVENTIONS

PLURAL NOUN _____

ADJECTIVE _____

ADJECTIVE _____

ADJECTIVE _____

TYPE OF LIQUID _____

PLURAL NOUN _____

PLURAL NOUN _____

PLURAL NOUN _____

ADJECTIVE _____

NOUN _____

PLURAL NOUN _____

PLURAL NOUN _____

PLURAL NOUN _____

ADJECTIVE _____

A PLACE _____

A PLACE _____

PART OF THE BODY _____

MAD LIBS
DR. COCKROACH'S
AMAZING INVENTIONS

Dr. Cockroach has invented many incredible _____ in his
PLURAL NOUN

lifetime. But most of them have been kept a/an _____
ADJECTIVE

secret by our _____ government. Here is a top secret list
ADJECTIVE

of some of his most _____ creations:
ADJECTIVE

• Glasses made out of _____ and _____ that
TYPE OF LIQUID   PLURAL NOUN

use _____ to help you see through _____
PLURAL NOUN   PLURAL NOUN

• A/An _____ time machine that runs on _____
ADJECTIVE   NOUN

juice and is made out of recycled _____ and
PLURAL NOUN

old _____
PLURAL NOUN

• A device constructed out of _____ that uses _____
PLURAL NOUN   ADJECTIVE

lasers to help people travel from (the) _____ to (the)
A PLACE

_____ in the blink of a/an _____
A PLACE   PART OF THE BODY

FROM MONSTERS VS. ALIENS™ MAD LIBS® • Monsters vs. Aliens ™ & © 2009 DreamWorks Animation L.L.C.
Published by Price Stern Sloan, a division of Penguin Young Readers Group, 345 Hudson Street, New York, NY 10014.

MAD LIBS® is fun to play with friends, but you can also play it by yourself! To begin with, DO NOT look at the story on the page below. Fill in the blanks on this page with the words called for. Then, using the words you have selected, fill in the blank spaces in the story.

Now you've created your own hilarious MAD LIBS® game!

THE MONSTER FILES: B.O.B.

SILLY WORD _____

ADJECTIVE _____

NOUN _____

ADJECTIVE _____

NOUN _____

PART OF THE BODY _____

ADVERB _____

ADJECTIVE _____

PART OF THE BODY _____

PLURAL NOUN _____

NOUN _____

ADJECTIVE _____

PLURAL NOUN _____

NOUN _____

ADJECTIVE _____

PLURAL NOUN _____

THE MONSTER FILES: B.O.B.

B.O.B., which stands for Benzoate _____ Bicarbonate,
SILLY WORD

was created when _____ scientists at a food plant
ADJECTIVE

combined a tomato with a/an _____-flavored dessert
NOUN

topping. The resulting _____ goop came to life as B.O.B.
ADJECTIVE

This gelatinous _____ can speak even though he has
NOUN

no _____. He is _____ indestructible, he
PART OF THE BODY ADVERB

has the _____ ability to fall from great heights and
ADJECTIVE

come out without a scratch on his _____, and he can
PART OF THE BODY

spatter into a million _____ only to re-form as a single
PLURAL NOUN

_____. He also has a/an _____ appetite and
NOUN ADJECTIVE

can consume large numbers of _____ at a time. B.O.B.
PLURAL NOUN

may not be the brightest _____ in the shed, but what
NOUN

this _____ blob lacks in brains, he makes up for in
ADJECTIVE

_____.
PLURAL NOUN

MAD LIBS® is fun to play with friends, but you can also play it by yourself! To begin with, DO NOT look at the story on the page below. Fill in the blanks on this page with the words called for. Then, using the words you have selected, fill in the blank spaces in the story.

Now you've created your own hilarious MAD LIBS® game!

MONSTERS VS. ALIENS, PART 1

NOUN _____

ADJECTIVE _____

NOUN _____

ADJECTIVE _____

NOUN _____

PLURAL NOUN _____

PART OF THE BODY (PLURAL) _____

ADJECTIVE _____

ADJECTIVE _____

VERB ENDING IN "ING" _____

ADJECTIVE _____

PLURAL NOUN _____

VERB _____

PLURAL NOUN _____

MAD LIBS
MONSTERS VS. ALIENS, PART 1

I am Gallaxhar, the most supreme alien _____ in
NOUN

the universe, and I believe that aliens are far better than boring,

_____ monsters. Here's why:
ADJECTIVE

• Aliens come from outer _____. We live on unique,
NOUN

_____ planets all over the universe. Monsters only live
ADJECTIVE

on that mud-covered _____, Earth.
NOUN

• Aliens are way smarter than _____. Just look at our
PLURAL NOUN

gigantic _____. These noggins hold some
PART OF THE BODY (PLURAL)

_____ brains!
ADJECTIVE

• Aliens have access to _____ technology that far surpasses
ADJECTIVE

anything monsters can use. For example, we can fly around in

_____ saucers, we have _____ robots
VERB ENDING IN "ING"   ADJECTIVE

and _____ to help us _____, and we get to
PLURAL NOUN   VERB

use cool weapons, like laser _____. You can't beat that!
PLURAL NOUN

MAD LIBS® is fun to play with friends, but you can also play it by yourself! To begin with, DO NOT look at the story on the page below. Fill in the blanks on this page with the words called for. Then, using the words you have selected, fill in the blank spaces in the story.

Now you've created your own hilarious MAD LIBS® game!

MONSTERS VS. ALIENS, PART 2

NOUN _____

NUMBER _____

ADJECTIVE _____

NOUN _____

A PLACE _____

ADJECTIVE _____

VERB _____

VERB ENDING IN "ING" _____

PLURAL NOUN _____

ADJECTIVE _____

ADJECTIVE _____

NOUN _____

ADJECTIVE _____

PLURAL NOUN _____

MAD LIBS
MONSTERS VS. ALIENS, PART 2

Hello there. The Missing Link here. There's no _____
<small>NOUN</small>

about it: Monsters are _____ times better than aliens.
<small>NUMBER</small>

Want some reasons? It's simple:

• Each monster is one of a kind. Take little, _____ me,
<small>ADJECTIVE</small>

for example. I'm the only part fish, part _____ in (the)
<small>NOUN</small>

_____.
<small>A PLACE</small>

• Monsters are cooler than _____ aliens. *Everyone* wants
<small>ADJECTIVE</small>

to _____ like us. Just take a look at what humans wear
<small>VERB</small>

trick-or-_____ on Halloween—there are way
<small>VERB ENDING IN "ING"</small>

more _____ dressed like monsters than aliens!
<small>PLURAL NOUN</small>

• Monsters have _____ strength and _____
<small>ADJECTIVE</small> <small>ADJECTIVE</small>

abilities. We're tougher than any _____ in the
<small>NOUN</small>

universe. Meanwhile, aliens are so weak, they need the help of

_____ blasters and _____ just to fight us.
<small>ADJECTIVE</small> <small>PLURAL NOUN</small>

MAD LIBS® is fun to play with friends, but you can also play it by yourself! To begin with, DO NOT look at the story on the page below. Fill in the blanks on this page with the words called for. Then, using the words you have selected, fill in the blank spaces in the story.

Now you've created your own hilarious MAD LIBS® game!

THE MONSTER FILES:
THE MISSING LINK

PLURAL NOUN _____

NOUN _____

PLURAL NOUN _____

PART OF THE BODY _____

ADJECTIVE _____

NOUN _____

ADVERB _____

ADJECTIVE _____

ADVERB _____

NUMBER _____

ADJECTIVE _____

NOUN _____

PLURAL NOUN _____

NOUN _____

PLURAL NOUN _____

NOUN _____

ADJECTIVE _____

ADJECTIVE _____

MAD LIBS
THE MONSTER FILES:
THE MISSING LINK

The Missing Link is twenty thousand _____ old. He is part
                                        PLURAL NOUN

fish, part _____. He has humanlike _____,
            NOUN   PLURAL NOUN

a scaly _____, and _____ flippers for
         PART OF THE BODY   ADJECTIVE

feet. Scientists recently discovered The Missing Link frozen

in a/an _____. Once they thawed him out, he
          NOUN

_____ escaped and caused _____ chaos. But
   ADVERB   ADJECTIVE

the government _____ captured him and placed
                   ADVERB

him in Area _____. This _____ monster
                NUMBER   ADJECTIVE

is a macho _____ who seems to think he's tougher
             NOUN

than _____. But the reality is, he can barely lift a/an
       PLURAL NOUN

_____. In fact, he couldn't run twenty _____
   NOUN   PLURAL NOUN

if his _____ depended on it. But regardless, he's still
         NOUN

a/an _____ show-off. Luckily for The Missing Link,
       ADJECTIVE

the other monsters at Area Fifty-Something like him despite his

_____ personality.
   ADJECTIVE

FROM MONSTERS VS. ALIENS™ MAD LIBS® • Monsters vs. Aliens ™ & © 2009 DreamWorks Animation L.L.C.
Published by Price Stern Sloan, a division of Penguin Young Readers Group, 345 Hudson Street, New York, NY 10014.

MAD LIBS® is fun to play with friends, but you can also play it by yourself! To begin with, DO NOT look at the story on the page below. Fill in the blanks on this page with the words called for. Then, using the words you have selected, fill in the blank spaces in the story.

Now you've created your own hilarious MAD LIBS® game!

DEAR DIARY, AGAIN

ADJECTIVE _____

ADJECTIVE _____

ADJECTIVE _____

PLURAL NOUN _____

ADJECTIVE _____

OCCUPATION _____

ADJECTIVE _____

PART OF THE BODY _____

ADJECTIVE _____

ADJECTIVE _____

NOUN _____

NOUN _____

ADJECTIVE _____

VERB ENDING IN "ING" _____

ADJECTIVE _____

NOUN _____

MAD LIBS

DEAR DIARY, AGAIN

Derek broke my _____ heart. To help get over our
                    ADJECTIVE

_____ breakup, I made a/an _____ list of his
   ADJECTIVE   ADJECTIVE

positive and negative _____.
                         PLURAL NOUN

Pros:

- He is tall, _____, and handsome.
                 ADJECTIVE

- He has a good job as a/an _____ for the
                                   OCCUPATION

_____ news.
   ADJECTIVE

Cons:

- He spends all day staring at his _____ in the mirror.
                                    PART OF THE BODY

- He cares more about his _____ job than his
                              ADJECTIVE

_____ fiancée.
   ADJECTIVE

- He said I was the _____ of his life. But now he
                         NOUN

wants to break off our _____ just because I'm a/an
                            NOUN

_____ giant.
   ADJECTIVE

I guess Derek's not the Prince _____ I thought he was.
                                VERB ENDING IN "ING"

I think I'm better off without that _____ _____.
                                       ADJECTIVE   NOUN

FROM MONSTERS VS. ALIENS™ MAD LIBS® • Monsters vs. Aliens ™ & © 2009 DreamWorks Animation L.L.C.
Published by Price Stern Sloan, a division of Penguin Young Readers Group, 345 Hudson Street, New York, NY 10014.

MAD LIBS® is fun to play with friends, but you can also play it by yourself! To begin with, DO NOT look at the story on the page below. Fill in the blanks on this page with the words called for. Then, using the words you have selected, fill in the blank spaces in the story.

Now you've created your own hilarious MAD LIBS® game!

ALIEN INVASION STOPPED BY MONSTERS!

ADJECTIVE _____

SILLY WORD _____

ADJECTIVE _____

ADVERB _____

ADJECTIVE _____

ADJECTIVE _____

PLURAL NOUN _____

A PLACE _____

ADJECTIVE _____

NOUN _____

VERB ENDING IN "ING" _____

ADJECTIVE _____

ADJECTIVE _____

VERB (PAST TENSE) _____

ADVERB _____

ADJECTIVE _____

MAD LIBS®
ALIEN INVASION STOPPED BY MONSTERS!

MODESTO, CA—A/An _____ group of monsters saved
                        ADJECTIVE

the world yesterday when an alien named _____ tried to
                                          SILLY WORD

take over Earth. The incident began when a/an _____
                                                ADJECTIVE

spaceship landed in Modesto, _____ abducting monster
                              ADVERB

Ginormica. According to _____ sources, Gallaxhar
                          ADJECTIVE

wanted to extract a/an _____ substance from her so
                        ADJECTIVE

he could create an army of _____. Gallaxhar then sent
                            PLURAL NOUN

giant robots to Paris, Tokyo, and (the) _____, where he
                                         A PLACE

planned to release his _____ clone army to help with
                        ADJECTIVE

his takeover. Meanwhile, three monsters—Dr. _____, The
                                              NOUN

_____ Link, and B.O.B.—were able to sneak aboard his
VERB ENDING IN "ING"

spaceship, find Ginormica, and defeat the _____ alien.
                                            ADJECTIVE

Another monster, Insectosaurus, flew his _____ friends
                                          ADJECTIVE

to safety just before the spaceship _____. President
                                     VERB (PAST TENSE)

Hathaway is expected to _____ thank the monsters in
                         ADVERB

a/an _____ address to the nation later today.
      ADJECTIVE

MAD LIBS® is fun to play with friends, but you can also play it by yourself! To begin with, DO NOT look at the story on the page below. Fill in the blanks on this page with the words called for. Then, using the words you have selected, fill in the blank spaces in the story.

Now you've created your own hilarious MAD LIBS® game!

INSECTOSAURUS LIVES!

NOUN _____

ADJECTIVE _____

PART OF THE BODY _____

NOUN _____

ADJECTIVE _____

ADJECTIVE _____

VERB ENDING IN "ING" _____

ADJECTIVE _____

NOUN _____

ADJECTIVE _____

PART OF THE BODY _____

ADJECTIVE _____

NOUN _____

ADJECTIVE _____

ADJECTIVE _____

PLURAL NOUN _____

MAD LIBS

INSECTOSAURUS LIVES!

When Gallaxhar abducted Ginormica, Insectosaurus made a heroic

_____ to rescue her. He shot a stream of _____
        NOUN   ADJECTIVE

silk out of his _____ and caught Ginormica with it. But
                      PART OF THE BODY

before he could pull her to safety, Gallaxhar zapped him with a

laser _____. The monsters thought Insectosaurus was
          NOUN

_____. A/An _____ cocoon wrapped around
    ADJECTIVE   ADJECTIVE

him, and the monsters left to save Ginormica. Little did they know,

he was still alive and _____. When General Monger
                   VERB ENDING IN "ING"

found Insectosaurus, he was no longer a/an _____
                                       ADJECTIVE

grub. Instead, he had become a beautiful winged _____.
                                            NOUN

General Monger got a/an _____ idea. He hopped on
                      ADJECTIVE

Insectosaurus's _____ and flew up to Gallaxhar's
             PART OF THE BODY

_____ spaceship just in the nick of _____ to
  ADJECTIVE   NOUN

rescue the _____ monsters. Not only did Insectosaurus
            ADJECTIVE

turn into a/an _____ butterfly—he saved his friends'
              ADJECTIVE

_____!
PLURAL NOUN

MAD LIBS® is fun to play with friends, but you can also play it by yourself! To begin with, DO NOT look at the story on the page below. Fill in the blanks on this page with the words called for. Then, using the words you have selected, fill in the blank spaces in the story.

Now you've created your own hilarious MAD LIBS® game!

THE MONSTER FILES:
DR. COCKROACH

ADJECTIVE _____

PERSON IN ROOM _____

PLURAL NOUN _____

ADJECTIVE _____

ADJECTIVE _____

PLURAL NOUN _____

ADJECTIVE _____

NOUN _____

PLURAL NOUN _____

ADJECTIVE _____

ADJECTIVE _____

PLURAL NOUN _____

ADJECTIVE _____

ADJECTIVE _____

ADJECTIVE _____

PART OF THE BODY _____

LAST NAME _____

Dr. Cockroach used to be a/an _____ scientist named
                                     ADJECTIVE

_____. He was one of the smartest _____
PERSON IN ROOM   PLURAL NOUN

on the planet, always creating _____ new inventions. He
                                    ADJECTIVE

was trying to invent a/an _____ machine that would
                                ADJECTIVE

make human _____ as indestructible as _____
                PLURAL NOUN   ADJECTIVE

cockroaches, when the invention turned the scientist into a/an

_____. Now, as Dr. Cockroach, he crawls up _____
    NOUN   PLURAL NOUN

and eats _____ garbage. But he still works on many
              ADJECTIVE

_____ inventions, using whatever _____
    ADJECTIVE   PLURAL NOUN

he can find. He is also _____ with computers and
                              ADJECTIVE

_____ technology. This _____ specimen's
    ADJECTIVE   ADJECTIVE

brilliant _____ may one day wind up on display in the
              PART OF THE BODY

famous _____ Museum.
            LAST NAME

FROM MONSTERS VS. ALIENS™ MAD LIBS® • Monsters vs. Aliens ™ & © 2009 DreamWorks Animation L.L.C.
Published by Price Stern Sloan, a division of Penguin Young Readers Group, 345 Hudson Street, New York, NY 10014.

MAD LIBS® is fun to play with friends, but you can also play it by yourself! To begin with, DO NOT look at the story on the page below. Fill in the blanks on this page with the words called for. Then, using the words you have selected, fill in the blank spaces in the story.

Now you've created your own hilarious MAD LIBS® game!

INTERVIEW WITH A MONSTER

ADJECTIVE _____

PERSON IN ROOM _____

ADVERB _____

NOUN _____

ADJECTIVE _____

PLURAL NOUN _____

NOUN _____

NOUN _____

PART OF THE BODY _____

PLURAL NOUN _____

NOUN _____

ADJECTIVE _____

PLURAL NOUN _____

ADJECTIVE _____

NOUN _____

MAD LIBS®

INTERVIEW WITH A MONSTER

The following is a television interview between The Missing Link

and _____ talk-show host, _____.
  　　　　　ADJECTIVE　　　　　　　　　　　　　PERSON IN ROOM

Host: Now that you've _____ saved Earth from an alien
  　　　　　　　　　　　　　ADVERB

_____, you've become a/an _____ celebrity.
  　　NOUN　　　　　　　　　　　　　　　　ADJECTIVE

How does it feel?

The Missing Link: I feel like a million _____. I was
  　　　　　　　　　　　　　　　　　　　PLURAL NOUN

hidden away in a government _____ for so long. I'm
  　　　　　　　　　　　　　　NOUN

really enjoying the _____-light.
  　　　　　　　　NOUN

Host: What went through your _____ when you fought
  　　　　　　　　　　　　　PART OF THE BODY

the alien clones?

The Missing Link: I felt sorry for those _____. They didn't
  　　　　　　　　　　　　　　　　　　PLURAL NOUN

stand a/an _____ against me.
  　　　　NOUN

Host: What are you going to do next?

The Missing Link: I'd like to write a/an _____ book
  　　　　　　　　　　　　　　　　　　ADJECTIVE

about my incredible _____. I'll call it _____
  　　　　　　　　PLURAL NOUN　　　　　　　　　　ADJECTIVE

Monster: My Amazing Life as a/an _____.
  　　　　　　　　　　　　　　　NOUN

MAD LIBS® is fun to play with friends, but you can also play it by yourself! To begin with, DO NOT look at the story on the page below. Fill in the blanks on this page with the words called for. Then, using the words you have selected, fill in the blank spaces in the story.

Now you've created your own hilarious MAD LIBS® game!

HOME, SWEET MONSTROUS HOME

ADJECTIVE _____

ADJECTIVE _____

A PLACE _____

ADJECTIVE _____

NOUN _____

PLURAL NOUN _____

ADJECTIVE _____

ADJECTIVE _____

NOUN _____

NOUN _____

NOUN _____

TYPE OF LIQUID _____

VERB _____

ADJECTIVE _____

ADJECTIVE _____

PLURAL NOUN _____

MAD LIBS®

HOME, SWEET MONSTROUS HOME

Are you a/an _____ monster in search of the perfect
                    ADJECTIVE

home? The _____ Community for Monsters might be
                ADJECTIVE

the place for you! Located in the middle of (the) _____,
                                                    A PLACE

the Community for Monsters is peaceful and _____. The
                                              ADJECTIVE

weather is always sunny, without a/an _____ in sight.
                                          NOUN

And everything is built especially for _____ of all sizes.
                                        PLURAL NOUN

There are many _____ activities to keep you entertained.
                  ADJECTIVE

Spend a/an _____ afternoon in an explosion-proof
              ADJECTIVE

_____ working on your latest _____. Go for
      NOUN   NOUN

a swim in a _____ filled with cool _____. Or,
                NOUN   TYPE OF LIQUID

if you're feeling hungry, enjoy the all-you-can-_____ buffet.
                                                    VERB

The best part is, you'll be surrounded by other _____
                                                    ADJECTIVE

monsters. Sound too good to be _____? It's not! Don't
                                  ADJECTIVE

delay. Call 1-800-_____ and buy your home today!
                    PLURAL NOUN